John Adams

GRAND PIANOLA MUSIC

Full Score

Part I 1
Part II: On the Dominant Divide 84

AMP-7995
First printing: June 1994

Associated Music Publishers, Inc.

7777 W. BLUEMOUND RD. P.O. BOX 13819 MILWAUKEE, WI 53213

PROGRAM NOTE

Of all my works, *Grand Pianola Music* has the most checkered past. It suffered through a tortured beginning, endured endless rewrites, has on all too many occasions been subjected to excruciatingly bad performances, and continues, even after ten years, to arouse the most divided responses from audiences. The piece, as the saying goes, seems to have something to offend everybody. Even so, and without being coy, I can say quite frankly that I wrote the piece not to *epater les bourgeoisie,* but rather for the sheer pleasure of hearing certain musical "signals"—one could even call them cliches—piled up against one another. Duelling pianos, cooing sirens, Valhalla brass, thwacking bass drums, gospel triads, and a Niagara of cascading flat keys all learned to cohabit as I wrote the piece.

As with my *Harmonielehre,* which began with a dream of a huge oil tanker rising like a Saturn rocket out of the waters of San Francisco Bay, *Grand Pianola Music* also started with a dream image in which, while driving down Interstate 5, I was approached from behind by two long, gleaming, black stretch limousines. As the vehicles drew up beside me they transformed into the world's longest Steinways...twenty, maybe even thirty feet long. Screaming down the highway at 90 m.p.h., they gave off volleys of B♭ and E♭ major arpeggios. I was reminded of walking down the hallways of the San Francisco Conservatory of Music, where I used to teach, hearing the sonic blur of twenty or more pianos playing Chopin, the *Emperor Concerto,* Hanon, Rachmaninoff, the *Maple Leaf Rag,* and much more.

Despite the image that inspired it, and despite the heft of its instrumentation (winds, brass, percussion, two bass drums, and, of course, the grand pianos), *Grand Pianola Music* is, for the most part, a surprisingly delicate piece. The woodwinds putter along in a most unthreatening fashion while waves of rippling piano arpeggiation roll in and out like tides. Three female voices (the sirens) sing wordless harmony, sometimes floating above the band in long sostenuto triads, while at other times imitating the crisp staccato of the winds and brass.

The principal technique of the piano writing was suggested to me by tape and digital delays, where a sound can be repeated in a fraction of a second. The two-piano version of this kind of delay was accomplished by having both pianists play essentially the same material, but with one slightly behind the other, usually a sixteenth or an eighth note apart. This gives the piano writing its unique shimmer.

Grand Pianola Music is in two parts, the first being, in fact, two movements, joined together without pause, that end up in a slow serene pasture with a grazing tuba. The shorter second part, "On the Dominant Divide," was an experiment in applying my minimalist techniques to the barest of all possible chord progressions, I-V-I. I had noticed that most "classical" minimalist pieces always progressed by motion of thirds in the bass and in all cases strictly avoided tonic-dominant relations, which are too fraught with a pressing need for resolution. What resulted was a swaying, rocking oscillation of phrases that gave birth to a melody. This tune, in the hero key of E♭ major, is repeated a number of times, and with each iteration it gains in gaudiness and Lisztian panache until it finally goes over the top to emerge in the gurgling C major of the lowest registers of the pianos. From here on it is a gradually accelerating race to the finish, with the tonalities flipping back and forth from major to minor, urging those gleaming black vehicles on to their final ecstasy.

—JOHN ADAMS

Instrumentation

2 Flutes (both doubling Piccolo)
2 Oboes
Clarinet in B♭ (2nd doubling Bass Clarinet)
2 Bassoons

2 Horns in F
2 Trumpets in B♭
2 Trombones
Tuba

Percussion (three players):
  Vibraphone, Xylophone, Marimba, Glockenspiel, Crotales, Bow (for Crotales),
  2 Suspended Cymbals, Crash Cymbals, 5 Tenor Drums, Small Pedal Bass Drum,
  Large Bass Drum, Maracas, High Wood Block, Tambourine, 2 Triangles

3 amplified women's voices

Piano 1
Piano 2

Duration: 30 minutes

Recordings:

*Electra/Nonesuch 79219 CD-2, The London Sinfonietta,
John Adams conductor, John Alley and Shelagh Sutherland, pianos*

*Angel CDC-47331-2, Solisti New York,
Ransom Wilson, conductor, Alan Feinberg and Ursula Oppens, pianos*

Commissioned by the General Atlantic Corporation and David M. Rumsey

*Premiere performance: February 26, 1982, The San Franciso Symphony,
John Adams, conductor, Robin Sutherland and Julie Steinberg, pianos*

Performance material is available on rental from the publisher.

GRAND PIANOLA MUSIC
Part I
John Adams

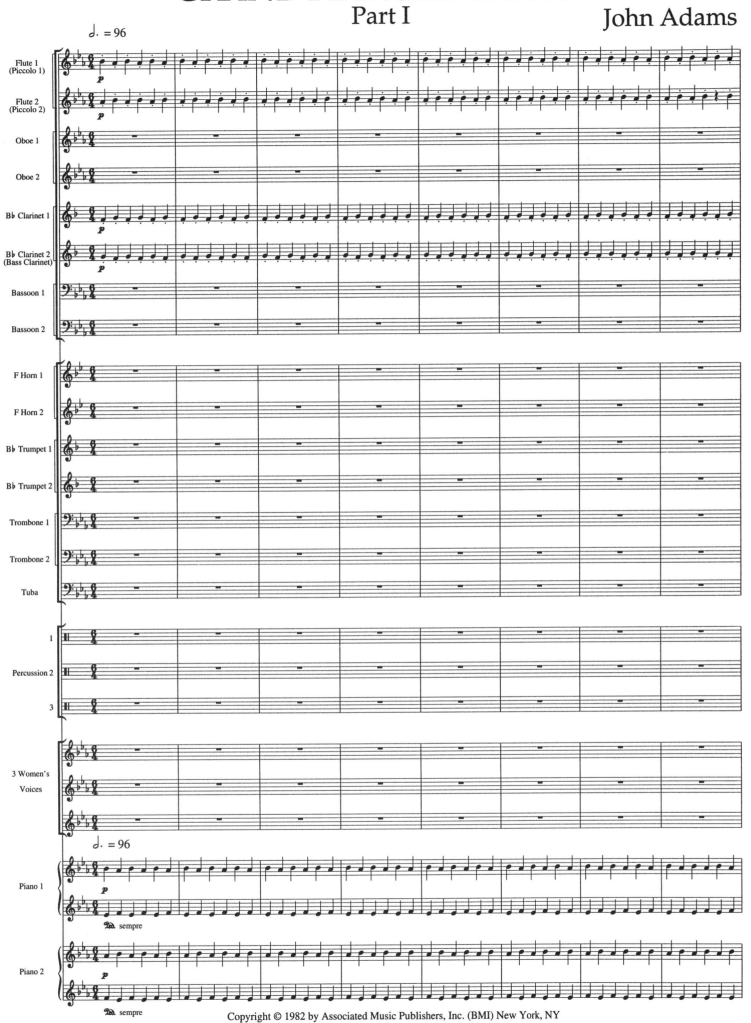

Copyright © 1982 by Associated Music Publishers, Inc. (BMI) New York, NY
International Copyright Secured. All Rights Reserved.
**Warning: Unauthorized reproduction of this publication is
prohibited by Federal law and subject to criminal prosecution.**

14

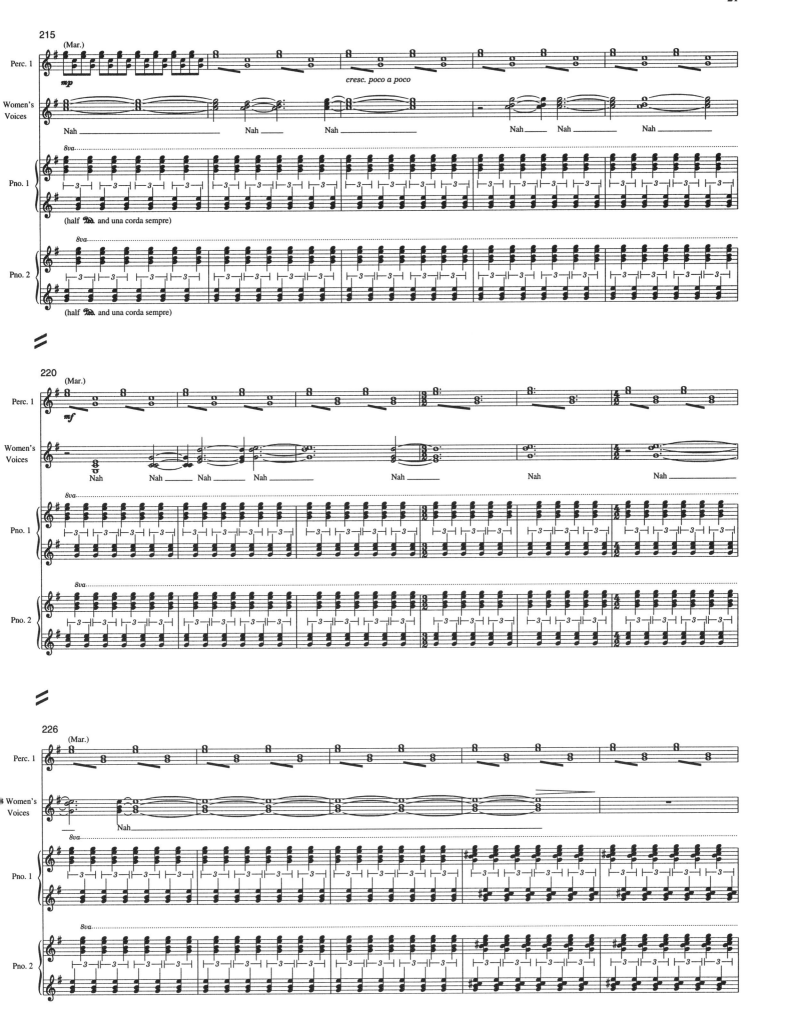

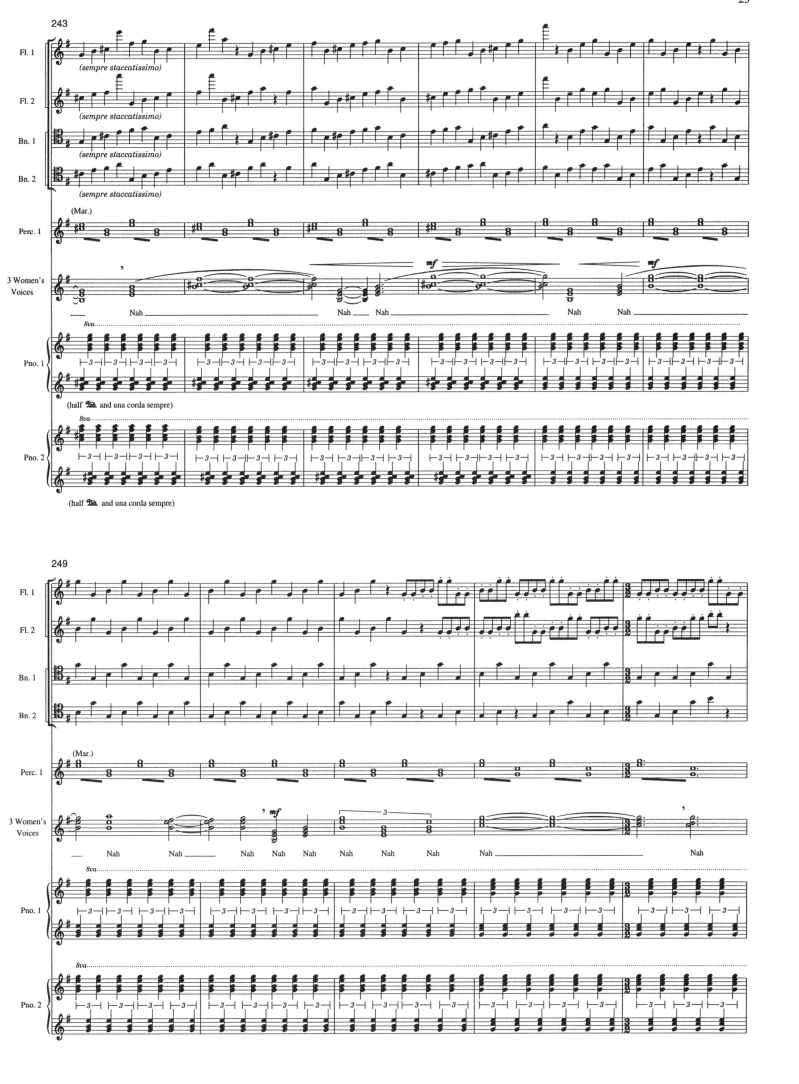

24

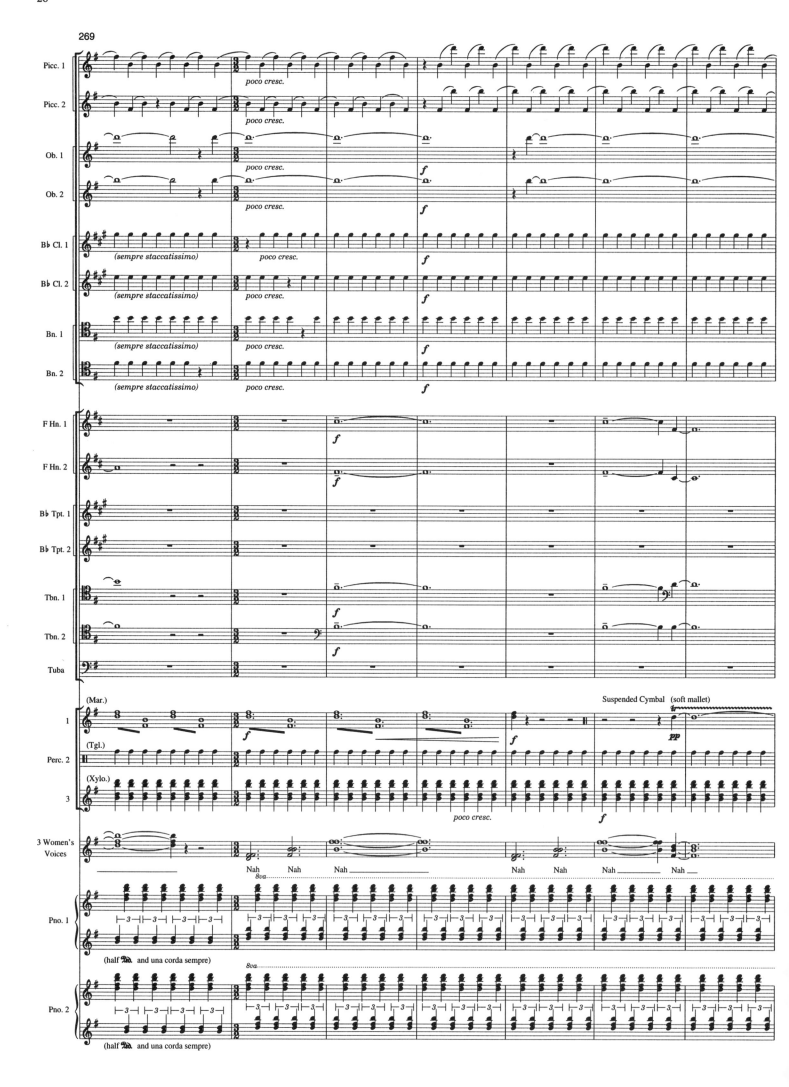

381

42

48

52

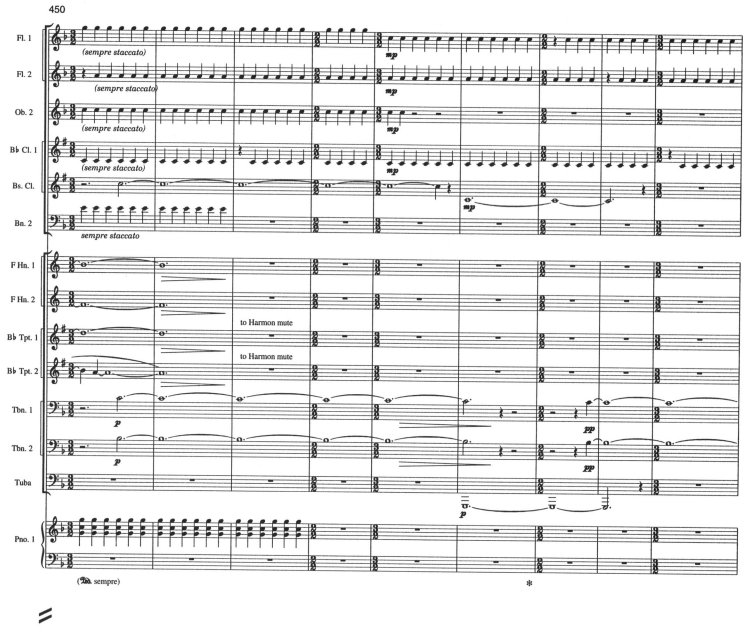

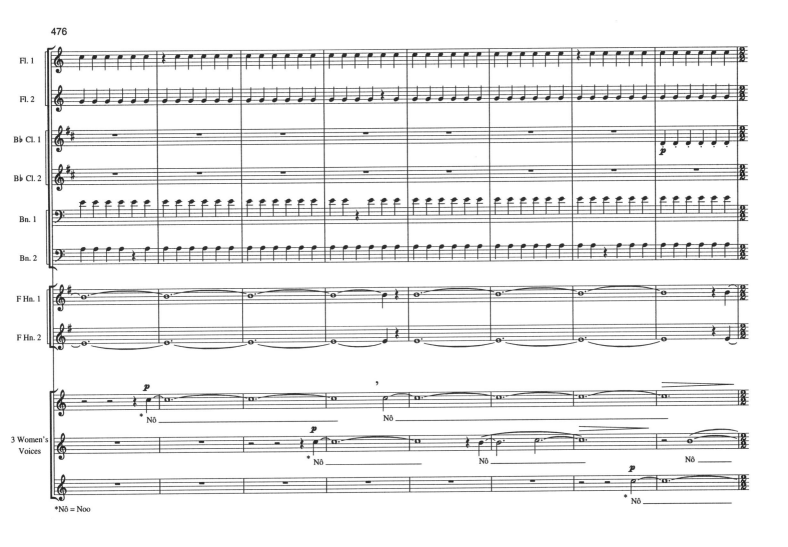

*Nô = Noo

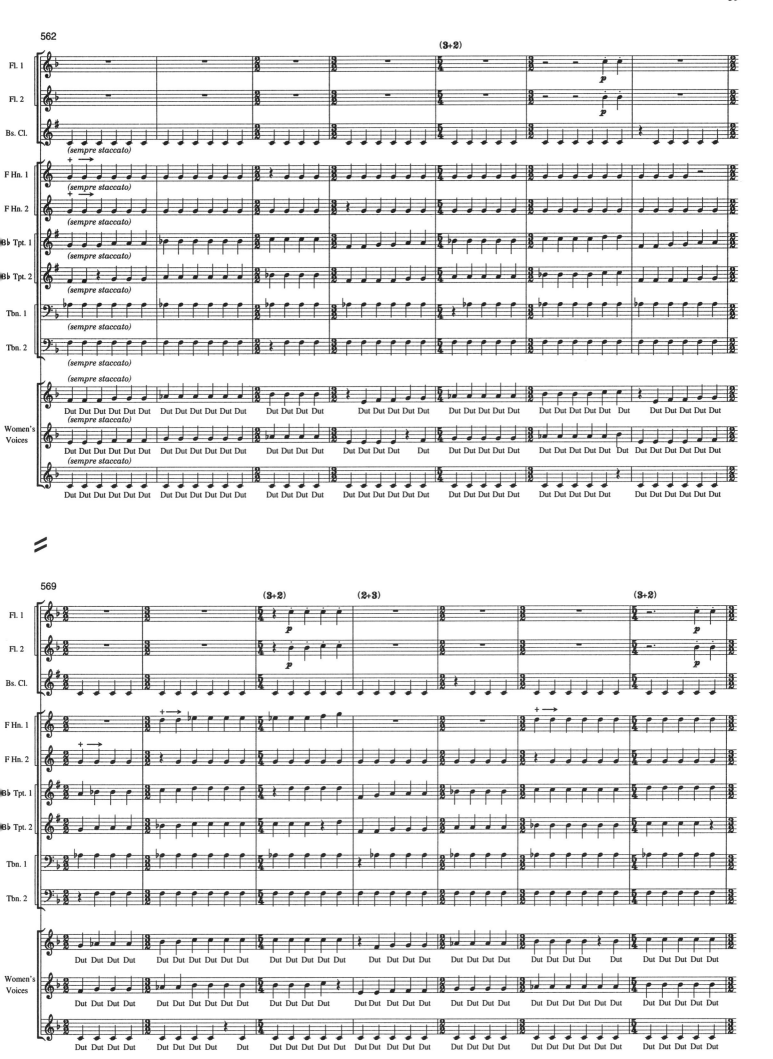

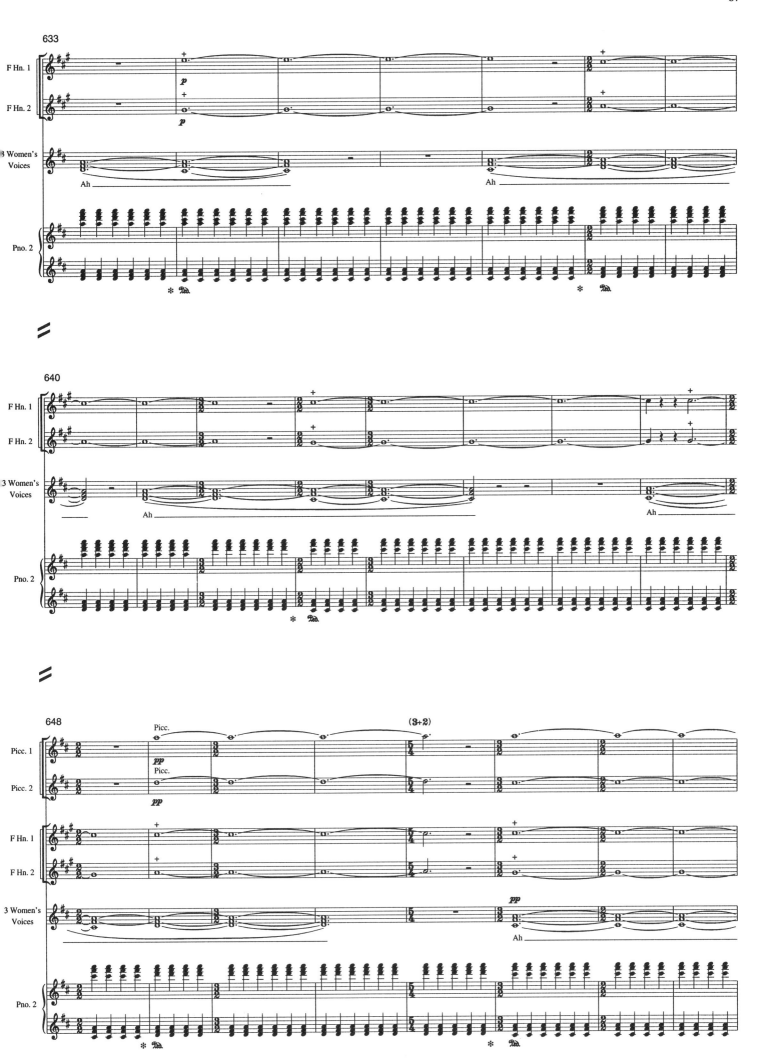

72

76

82

Part II: On the Dominant Divide

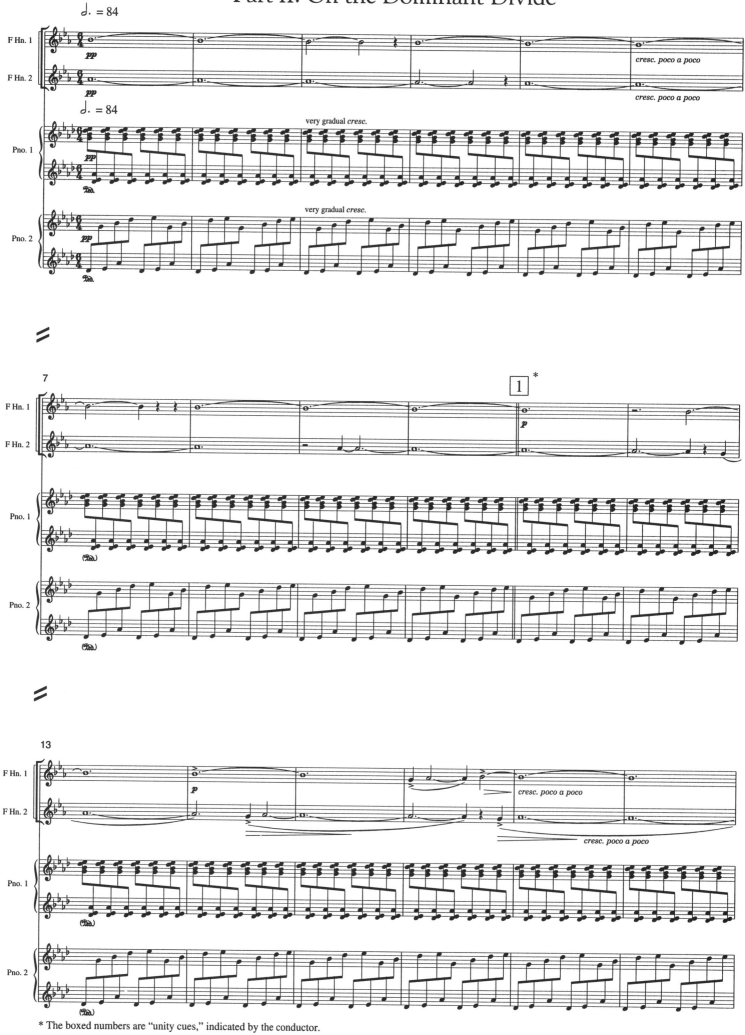

* The boxed numbers are "unity cues," indicated by the conductor.

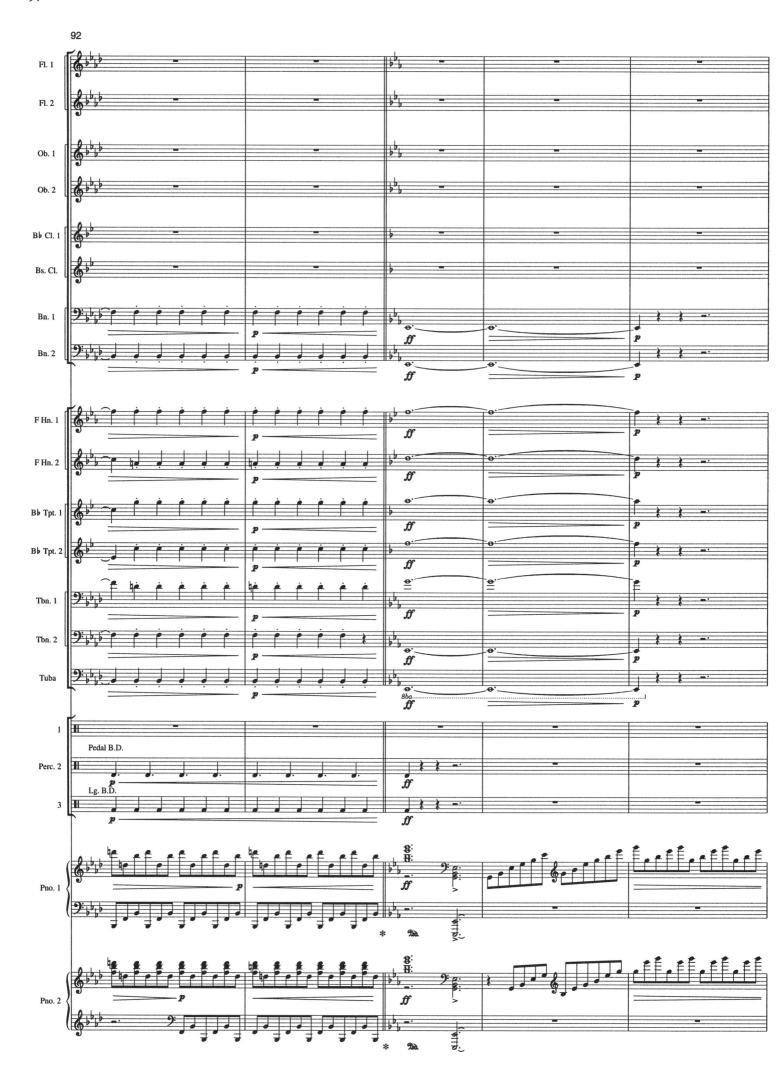

96

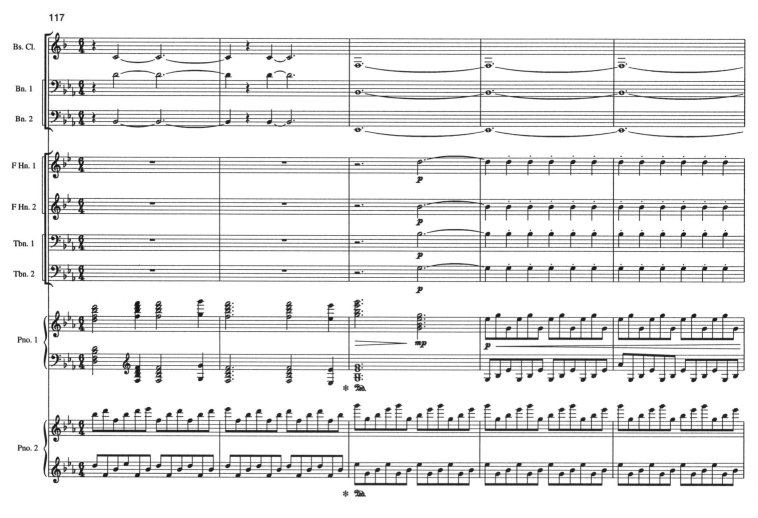

98

106

112

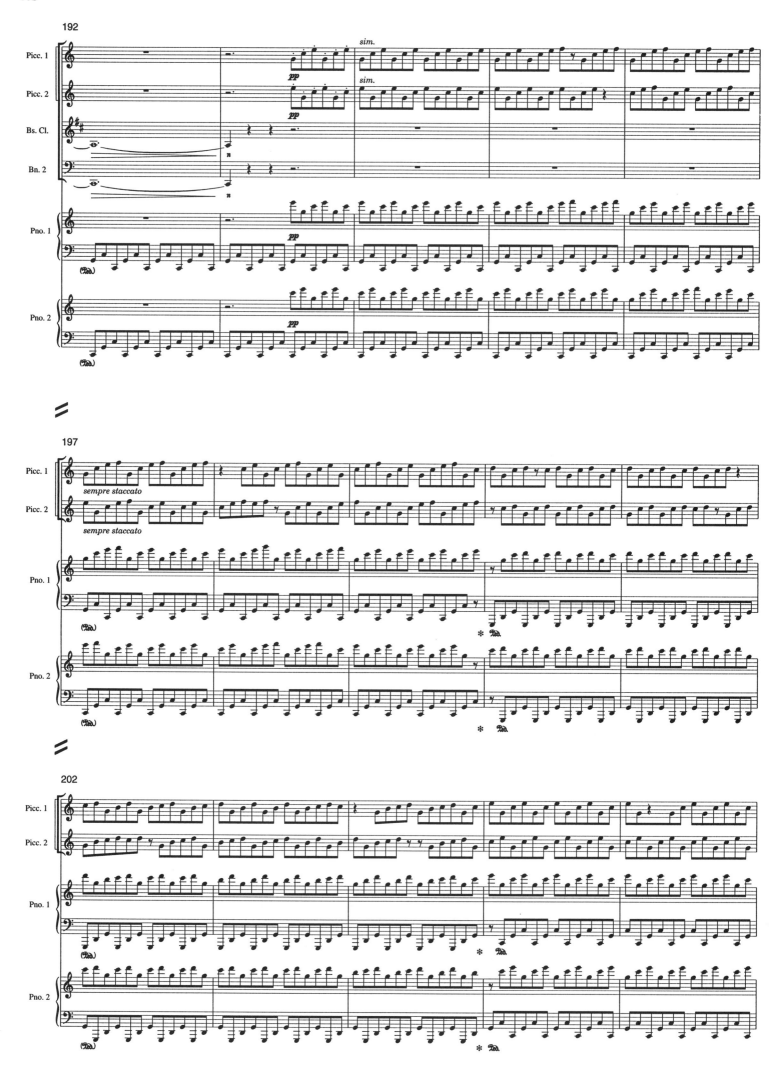

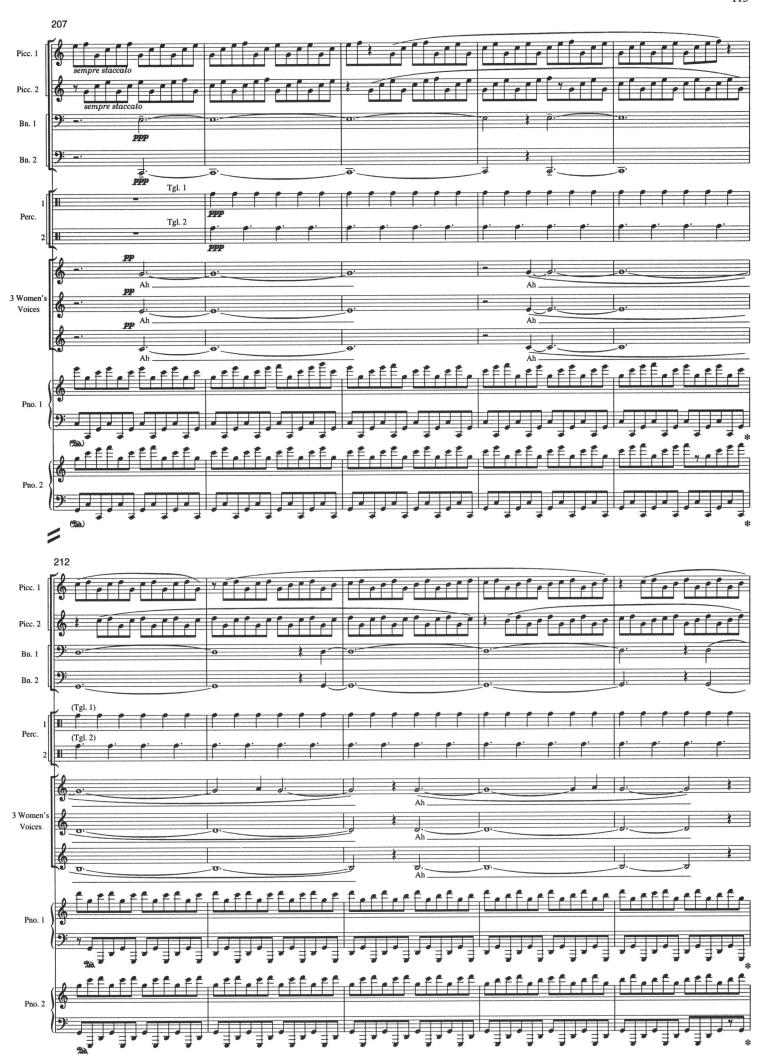

116

126